GREATER MANCHESTER BUSES 1986–2006

KEITH A. JENKINSON

AMBERLEY

First published 2022

Amberley Publishing
The Hill, Stroud
Gloucestershire, GL5 4EP

www.amberley-books.com

Copyright © Keith A. Jenkinson, 2022

The right of Keith A. Jenkinson to be identified
as the Author of this work has been asserted in
accordance with the Copyrights, Designs and
Patents Act 1988.

ISBN 978 1 3981 0938 4 (print)
ISBN 978 1 3981 0939 1 (ebook)

British Library Cataloguing in Publication Data.
A catalogue record for this book is available from
the British Library.

Origination by Amberley Publishing.
Printed in the UK.

Introduction

The county of Greater Manchester was created in 1974 as a consequence of the Local Government Act 1972, and as a result SELNEC was renamed Greater Manchester Transport and in 1981 it absorbed Lancashire United Transport. In 1986, following deregulation, Greater Manchester Transport was renamed GM Buses, and then on 31 December 1993 the company was split into two as GM Buses North and GM Buses South. Following this, in March 1994 both companies were sold to employee buyout teams, and two years later in the spring of 1996 were respectively sold to FirstBus and Stagecoach.

Manchester and its surrounds, including Bolton, Wigan, Rochdale, Oldham, Altrincham, and Stockport, has always been a haven for bus enthusiasts, with a wide variety of operators and liveries to be seen. Deregulation in 1986 changed the scene dramatically, however, with the appearance of numerous independent companies – some of which were short-lived while others survived for many years or were swallowed up by the major national conglomerates such as Arriva, FirstBus and Stagecoach. Added to the mix is the Metrolink tramway system, which opened in 1992 and continues to grow, having now reached the airport where numerous buses can also be seen.

It is believed that in 1989 there were sixty-eight bus/coach operators in Greater Manchester, amongst which were a few that had been in business since before deregulation in October 1986. Within this mix was, of course, Greater Manchester PTE (originally SELNEC PTE), which had subsumed all the eleven surrounding municipal companies on 1 November 1969 to give it a combined fleet of 2,532 buses. In addition there was Clayton-based Mayne, who was established in 1922 as a coaching company and had operated buses between Manchester and Ashton-under-Lyne since 1929; even older Finglands, Rusholme, who started in business in 1907 but did not venture into bus operation until 1986; and Walls, Fallowfield, who also began as a coach operator. In addition there was Ribble and North Western, who both operated into the area from surrounding towns.

Turning back to 1986, shortly before deregulation on 26 October, Citibus Tours of Chadderton, who had started as a coach company in 1979 and had competed with GM Buses on its Manchester Centreline route from 1983 to 1986, began a service to Blackley using ex-Isle of Man Transport Leyland Panthers, which had started life with Preston Borough Transport, and sold out to GM Buses North in 1995. Also joining the fray in 1986 was Cooper of Dukinfield, who later traded as Dennis' Coaches and expanded over the years until it was acquired by Stagecoach in September 2005. Shearings, Bolton; Stotts Tours, Oldham; Walsh (JP Travel), Middleton; Trimtrack,

Hyde, who became Stuarts; Central Coaches, Oldham; and Bullocks, Cheadle, all established coach operators who took the gamble to add local bus operation to their portfolios.

Almost before the dust had settled, several other entrepreneurs appeared on the scene, the largest being Manchester Minibuses, who, trading as Bee Line Buzz Company, in January 1987 introduced a fleet of bright yellow-liveried 'bread van' minibuses to the city and competed with the established operators until it sold out in 1988 to Ribble, who the following year disposed of it, together with its own Manchester operations, to Drawlane subsidiary North Western. Then, during the last years of the 1980s several more newcomers arrived on the scene, amongst whom was Sports Tours, Rochdale, who traded as Pioneer; Arrowline Travel (who traded as Star Line), Knutsford; Bluebird, Middleton; Vale of Manchester; Checkmate, Mossley (who later traded as Tandy Bus); and Eccles-based Lyntown Bus Company, who sold the company to Midway, Manchester, in April 1990. In addition, following its acquisition by ATL in 1988 and thence via National Express to the Drawlane Group, Crosville increased its presence in Manchester as too did Stevensons, Spath, while Stagecoach subsidiary East Midlands Motor Services launched its Frontrunner North West subsidiary around Stockport in 1988 and then sold it to Drawlane-owned North Western in September of the following year.

During the next decade, the flow of new independent operators continued at pace bringing even more new liveries and vehicles into an ever-fascinating scene. 1990 began with Bee Line Buzz's Macclesfield depot operations being set up as a standalone business under the title C-Line Bus Company before being transferred to Midland Red North management in 1992, as too was Stevensons two years later. Then, in 1991 several newcomers made their debut, amongst which were Blue Bus at Horwich; Tame Valley Motor Services; Pennine Blue, Ashton-under-Lyne; and Mybus, Hadfield. Of these, Blue Bus sold out to Arriva in 2005, Tame Valley was taken over in 1995 by Glossopdale, who in 1999 sold out to Stagecoach, Pennine Blue was acquired by Badgerline subsidiary PMT in 1994, while Mybus ceased trading in 1994 but a year later was reformed as UK North.

As the 1990s moved forward, several more new local bus operators made their debut, amongst which were Atherton Bus Company; Timeline, who took over Shearings stage carriage operations in 1992; Evag Cannon, Bolton; Glossopdale Bus Company, Dukinfield, in 1993; Wigan Bus Company, who began in 1993 and sold out to British Bus in 1995; Mancunian, who was associated with Midway from 1993 and operated ex-London Routemasters; South Manchester Transport, Hyde, in 1993; Bu-Val Buses, Littleborough; Universal Buses, Chadderton, in 1998; and Coachmasters, Rochdale, in 1999. However, these were comparative small fry when compared to another predator who entered Manchester in 1993: MTL, Liverpool, the former Merseyside PTE company, who began services competing with GM Buses North and GM Buses South who both launched retaliatory action in Merseyside. In Manchester, Bury and Rochdale, the new predator used the fleet names MTL Manchester, whereas in Wigan and Bolton MTL's St Helens depot operated as Lancashire Travel. After two years of battling, peace was eventually reached between MTL and GM Buses in 1995 when both returned to their old established territories. Meanwhile, as the 1990s progressed, Warrington Borough Transport and independent Bennetts both began to operate from Altrincham to Warrington while several of the larger companies such as Trent, Arriva and Stagecoach ran services from Buxton, Stockport and Altrincham to the airport under the Skyline banner. Then, in 1999 bendibuses made their first appearance when First Manchester introduced them on the service from Manchester to Bury.

The start of the new millennium initially saw little change, with the remaining independent operators still soldiering on, the Metrolink system continuing to expand, and Stagecoach introducing its new 'beach ball' livery, which gradually replaced its original stripes. However, much began to alter, with Stagecoach acquiring much of its opposition – Universal Buses (services only) in 2000; Walls and Dennis's in 2005; Bullocks and Mayne in 2008; Bluebird in 2013; and JPT Travel in 2014, although Walls, Bullocks and Mayne all retained their coaching operations. Not to be left out, Arriva acquired Blue Bus in 2005 while First purchased Pioneer in 2002 but sold its Wigan operations to Stagecoach in 2012 and its central Manchester operations to Go-Ahead in 2019. In the meantime, Speedwellbus, Hyde, appeared on the scene in 2002 while on the other side of the coin UK North ceased trading in 2007 as too did Vale of Manchester in 2008. Despite the disappearance of many of the old established and younger independent operators, new ones still keep appearing, and as such Manchester continues to be a fascinating city for transport enthusiasts with its variety of liveries and vehicles.

Although most of the operators to be seen in Greater Manchester between 1986 and 2005 have been mentioned or illustrated in this book, I accept that there are a few smaller ones that have been omitted and apologise for this. Hopefully this will not detract from the pleasure of readers, but there's a limit to what can be fitted into ninety-six pages. Enjoy.

Displaying a GM Buses fleet name, MCW Metrobus 5066 (MRJ 66W), which was new in April 1981, awaits its passengers in Piccadilly bus station, Manchester, on 15 August 1986. (K. A. Jenkinson)

Adorned with branding for route 68 and carrying a Greater Manchester Transport fleet name and logo, Northern Counties-bodied Leyland Olympian 3142 (B142 WNB), which began life in July 1985, is seen here in Piccadilly bus station, Manchester, on 15 August 1986. (K. A. Jenkinson)

Purchased for operation on Manchester's Centreline service, GM Buses Northern Counties-bodied Dennis Domino midibus 1766 (C766 YBA) collects two passengers at Piccadilly railway station on 15 August 1986 before crossing the city centre to Victoria rail station. (K. A. Jenkinson)

Wearing Citibus's original livery and seen here in Piccadilly bus station, Manchester, on 15 August 1986, a couple of months before deregulation, is Seddon-bodied 12 (RTF 436L), which was the last Leyland Panther built for a UK operator. Starting life with Preston Corporation in April 1973, in December 1984 it passed to Isle of Man Transport who re-registered it MAN7657, after which it was then purchased by Citibus in June 1986. (K. A. Jenkinson)

Bought new by Mayne, Manchester, in June 1978, immaculately presented Bristol VRT VJA 666S with coach-seated ECW body is pictured here in Piccadilly bus station, Manchester, on 15 August 1986. (K. A. Jenkinson)

Also seen in Piccadilly bus station, Manchester, on 15 August 1986 is Mayne's former London Park Royal-bodied Leyland Fleetline OJD 163R, which was new in December 1976 and was acquired by the Manchester independent in December 1982. (K. A. Jenkinson)

GM Buses Leyland Lynx 501 (D501 LNA), which was purchased new in December 1986, is seen here sporting a Rochdale identifier above its passenger entrance door. (Author's collection)

Heading along Market Street, Manchester, is Carlyle-bodied Freight Rover Sherpa D128 NON, which was new to Manchester Minibuses in January 1987 and still wears its original livery and Minilink name, beneath which is a Ribble strap line. (K. A. Jenkinson)

Seen in Bury bus station in August 1988 are Shearings ex-Greater Manchester PTE 1977 vintage Leyland National 54 (RBU 182R) and GM Buses Northern Counties-bodied Leyland Atlantean 8345 (MNC 545W), which was new in February 1981. (K. A. Jenkinson)

Departing Piccadilly, Manchester, for Ashton-under-Lyne on 3 October 1989 is independent Stuart's nicely presented Alexander-bodied Leyland Atlantean ABM 799A, which was new to Aberdeen Corporation in 1974, registered NRG 178M. (K. A. Jenkinson)

Heading along Mosley Street, Manchester, en route to Rochdale on 3 October 1989, is Crosville ECW-bodied Bristol VRT DVL383 (FTU 383T), which was new in August 1978. (K. A. Jenkinson)

New to Manchester Minibuses in March 1987, Carlyle-converted Freight Rover Sherpa D228 OOJ is seen here in Stockport bus station in October 1989 after to passing to Crosville and being given its Mini Lynx fleet name. Behind it is GM Buses Northern Counties-bodied Leyland Atlantean 8156 (VBA 156S), which was new in January 1978. (K. A. Jenkinson)

Stagecoach subsidiary East Midland briefly entered Greater Manchester under the Frontrunner North West name from a base at Tintwhistle. Seen here in Stockport bus station on 3 October 1989 is Plaxton-bodied Leyland Leopard 20 (ANU 20T), which had started life with East Midland in August 1978. (K. A. Jenkinson)

Leaving Stockport bus station on 3 October 1989 a few days after Frontrunner North West had been taken over by North Western, Alexander-bodied Leyland Atlantean 431 (KSA 178P) had started life with Grampian in January 1976. (K. A. Jenkinson)

Seen in Mosley Street, Manchester, on the 343 service to Altrincham on 3 October 1989, North Western Leyland National 2 273 (BVP 809V) was new to Midland Red in January 1980. (K. A. Jenkinson)

In August 1988 GM Buses bought ten AEC Routemasters from London Buses for operation on route 143 from Piccadilly to West Didsbury, which was branded the Piccadilly Line. Here 2201/ RM1136 (136 CLT) is seen in Mosley Street, Manchester, on 3 October 1989, but all were withdrawn for disposal in June of the following year. (K. A. Jenkinson)

Starting life with Eastern Counties in July 1970 registered XAH 871H, independent Lyntown Bus Company ECW-bodied Bristol RELL6G (MBU 388H) is seen here in Mosley Street, Manchester, operating a schools service on 3 October 1989. (K. A. Jenkinson)

Seen in Piccadilly, Manchester, in 1989 bound for Oldham is independent Central Coaches (Wild, Chadderton) ECW-bodied Bristol VRT (UWY 63L), which was new to York West Yorkshire, in March 1973 and is still wearing that operator's livery. (T. W. W. Knowles)

Leaving Piccadilly bus station, Manchester, on the 233 service to Carrbrook on 3 October 1989, Mayne's ex-GM Buses Northern Counties standard-bodied Daimler Fleetline WWH 54L was new to SELNEC in March 1973. (K. A. Jenkinson)

Resting in Ashton-under-Lyne bus station in October 1989 are PMT minilink-branded MHR424 (E724 HBF), a PMT-bodied Freight Rover Sherpa new in August 1987, and Crosville ECW-bodied Bristol VRT DVL383 (FTU 383T). (K. A. Jenkinson)

Heading through Manchester is independent Finglands Northern Counties-bodied Daimler
CRG6LXB 709 (WWH 53L), which began life with SELNEC in March 1973. (K. A. Jenkinson)

Departing from Piccadilly bus station, Manchester, on 11 August 1990 and still wearing
the livery of its previous owner Ribble, albeit with an added yellow lower front panel, is Bee
Line Park Royal-bodied Leyland Atlantean, behind which are three GM Buses double-deckers
including Northern Counties-bodied Leyland Atlantean 8404 (MRJ 404W). (K. A. Jenkinson)

Pictured in Ashton-under-Lyne bus station on 8 November 1990 is Stotts of Oldham Northern Counties-bodied Daimler Fleetline YNA 303M, which had been acquired from GM Buses who, as SELNEC, had purchased it new in May 1974. (K. A. Jenkinson)

Seen in Manchester on 11 November 1990 is Walsh of Middleton's Robin Hood-bodied Iveco 49.10 747 (D74 7ERV), which was new as a demonstrator for its coachbuilder in September 1987. Carrying the fleet name City Nipper, Walsh later changed its identity to JPT Travel. (K. A. Jenkinson)

Operating a schools service in 1990 is Stuart of Hyde's Plaxton-bodied Leyland Leopard RWU 535R, which began life with West Yorkshire PTE in October 1976. (B. Newsome)

C-Line Northern Counties-bodied Dodge S46 D415 NNA, which was new to Manchester Minibuses in April 1987, is seen here leaving Ashton-under-Lyne bus station on a journey to Stockport on 12 March 1991. (K. A. Jenkinson)

Seen in Ashton-under-Lyne bus station on 12 March 1991 heading a line of buses that included a Pennine Blue Bristol RELL and a GM Buses double-decker, Mayne of Manchester Leyland Leopard 22 (LIW 1322) was new to Poole, Alsagers Bank in September 1972. Carrying a Willowbrook coach body and registered NRE582L, it was given its new Willowbrook body in December 1990. (K. A. Jenkinson)

Resting between duties on 12 March 1991, Cooper of Dukinfield (who traded as Dennis's Coaches and was acquired by Stagecoach in 2005) Alexander-bodied Seddon Pennine 7 YSD 813T started life with Western SMT in November 1978. (K. A. Jenkinson)

Preparing to take up its next duty on the 333 service to Hattersley, Stuarts of Hyde's Park Royal-bodied Leyland Fleetline SDA 613S, which was new to West Midlands PTE in September 1977, is seen here in Ashton-under-Lyne bus station on 7 September 1991. (K. A. Jenkinson)

Having just arrived in Ashton-under-Lyne bus station from Manchester on route 216 on 7 September 1991 is C-Line's Gardner re-engined Leyland National SNG392 (GMB 392T), which was new to Crosville in December 1978. (K. A. Jenkinson)

Making its way through Piccadilly, Manchester, on 20 May 1992, is Bee Line Buzz Company Northern Counties-bodied Leyland Atlantean 664 (HJA 114N), which had started life with Greater Manchester PTE in February 1975. (K. A. Jenkinson)

Appearing to have been recently repainted and seen here in Manchester city centre on 20 May 1992 is C-Line ECW-bodied Leyland Atlantean SFV 428P, which had been new to Ribble in July 1976. (K. A. Jenkinson)

Making its way through its home city centre on 20 May 1992 on the 41X service to West Didsbury is local independent Vale of Manchester's Duple-bodied Leyland Leopard URN 153V, which had started life with Lancaster City Transport in September 1979. (K. A. Jenkinson)

Still wearing the livery of its former owner London & Country, to whom it was new in January 1979, but carrying the fleet name of its new custodian Bee Line Buzz Company, Roe-bodied Leyland Atlantean AN189 (XPG 189T) is seen here in Manchester on 20 May 1992. (K. A. Jenkinson)

Originating with London Country in December 1983 and seen here in Manchester on 20 May 1992 operated by C-Line, albeit still painted in in Green Line livery, is Plaxton Paramount-bodied Leyland Tiger TP18 (A11 8EPA). (K. A. Jenkinson)

Entering Piccadilly bus station, Manchester, on 20 May 1992, is Bullock of Cheadle's East Lancs-bodied Dennis Dominator 283 (C283 BBP), which began life with Southampton City Transport in July 1986. (K. A. Jenkinson)

Also in Market Street on 20 May 1992 amongst GM Buses double-deckers and a C-Line coach are two Rossendale vehicles: Carlyle-bodied Freight Rover Sherpa 53 (D953 NOJ), which was new to the borough council in October 1986, and East Lancs-bodied Leyland Atlantean 130 (VDY 530T), which it had acquired from Eastbourne Buses. (K. A. Jenkinson)

Having just left Piccadilly bus station, Manchester en route to Whitefield on 10 May 1992 is Citibus Roe-bodied Leyland Atlantean 640 (XWG 640T), which had started life with South Yorkshire PTE in November 1978. (K. A. Jenkinson)

Seen in Market Street, Manchester, on 20 May 1992, still wearing London livery is MCW-bodied Leyland Fleetline THX 342S which was new to London Transport in 1978, passed to Mybus, Hadfield, in December 1991, and was then sold via Ripley (dealer), Carlton, to Speedybus Enterprises, Hong Kong, in July 1993. (K. A. Jenkinson)

Purchased new by Shearings in February 1990 and seen here in Piccadilly, Manchester, on 20 May 1992 after passing to Timeline, is Alexander (Belfast)-bodied Leyland Tiger 68 (G68 RND). (K. A. Jenkinson)

Wearing a C-Line Midland Red fleet name on its side panels and painted in Midland Red North livery, Leyland National 859 (TPE 159S), which started life with Alder Valley, is seen here in Manchester in February 1993. (B. Newsome)

Pictured here is 1004A, one of Manchester Metrolink's original trams. New in April 1992, it was a T68 built in Italy by Firema, remained in service until 16 May 2012, and was scrapped two years later. (M. H. A. Flynn)

Starting life with South Yorkshire PTE in January 1987, Reeve Burgess-bodied Dodge S56 (D110 OWG) is seen here on 15 March 1993 leaving Stockport bus station after its acquisition by Glossopdale Bus Company. (K. A. Jenkinson)

Exiting Stockport bus station on 15 March 1993, C-Line's ECW-bodied Leyland Atlantean 2065 (NNO 65P), which was new to Colchester Borough Transport in May 1976, squeezes past Bullock of Cheadle's ex-London MCW-bodied Leyland Fleetline THX 272S, both of which are operating the 42 service to Manchester. (K. A. Jenkinson)

Entering Piccadilly bus station, Manchester, on 23 April 1993, followed by GM Buses Park Royal-bodied Leyland Atlantean 7919 (ANC 919T), is The Bee Line Buzz Company's Northern Counties-bodied Leyland Atlantean KDB 684P, which began life with Greater Manchester PTE in September 1975. (T. S. Blackman)

Turning into Manchester's Piccadilly bus station on 20 April 1993 is Mybus, Hadfield's recently acquired Park Royal-bodied Leyland Fleetline HD49 (THX 494S), which began life with London Transport in 1978 and was exported to Speedybus Enterprises (dealer), Hong Kong, after only four months service in Greater Manchester. (K. A. Jenkinson)

Owned by Manchester Airport where it is seen here when new in May 1993 operating on site shuttle services, is dual-door Ikarus-bodied DAF SB220 K127 TCP. (K. A. Jenkinson)

Also owned by Manchester Airport and used on terminal transfer duties is Optare Solo K976 JWW, which was new in July 1993 and is seen here when only a few weeks old. (K. A. Jenkinson)

Arriving at Manchester Airport from Altrincham in May 1993 is Arrowline of Knutsford (who traded as Star Line) Plaxton-bodied Mercedes Benz 709D J298 NNB. (K. A. Jenkinson)

Collecting its passengers at Manchester Airport and displaying an Airport Buslink logo on its upper side panels is GM Buses Northern Counties-bodied Dennis Dominator 2015 (B915 TVR). (K. A. Jenkinson)

Pictured in Bolton on 15 March 1993 is independent Evag Cannon's dual-door Leyland National BYW 372V, which was new to London Transport in September 1979. (K. A. Jenkinson)

Awaiting its passengers at Manchester Airport in April 1993, and wearing branding for its service from Accrington, is Hyndburn Transport's Duple-bodied Leyland Leopard 75 (MNK 421V), which had been purchased new by Fox, Hayes, in April 1980. (K. A. Jenkinson)

Parked at Pennine Blue's Dukinfield depot in 1993 is ex-Northern General dual-door ECW-bodied Leyland Atlantean 3297 (MPT 297P), which was new in November 1975. (K. A. Jenkinson)

Starting life with Western National in January 1971 and then passing to Chase of Chasetown and Independent Coachways, Horsforth, ECW-bodied Bristol RELL6G (TUO 263J) was acquired by Pennine Blue in February 1993 before ultimately being scrapped in November 1994. Numbered 63, it is seen here in the autumn of 1994. (K. A. Jenkinson)

Newcomer Mancunian Bus Company's AEC Routemaster RM149 (EDS 117A, originally VLT 149), which had previously been operated by Kelvin Scottish, stands at Midway's depot at Bradford, Manchester, in April 1993. (K. A. Jenkinson)

Resting between duties in Wigan on 9 April 1994 is ECW-bodied Bristol VRT 558 (RMA 439V), which had started life with Crosville in April 1980 and was transferred to North Western in November 1989. (K. A. Jenkinson)

Entering Wigan bus station on 4 April 1994 are two Merseybus MCW Metrobuses with Lancashire Travel fleet names, headed by 0801 (F801 YLV) sporting a makeshift destination display. Departing on the left is GM Buses Northern Counties-bodied Dodge S56 1987 (E987 SJA) with 'I'm your Little Gem' branding. (K. A. Jenkinson)

Sporting a Lancashire Travel fleet name, St Helens-based thirteen-year-old Merseybus Leyland National 2 7004 (XTJ 4W) is seen entering Wigan bus station on 9 April 1993. (K. A. Jenkinson)

Passing sister HSC 109T as it makes its way towards Wigan bus station on 9 April 1994 is Wigan Bus Company Leyland National HSC 112T, both buses having started life north of the border with Alexander Fife in October 1978. (K. A. Jenkinson)

Making its way past Wigan railway station on 9 April 1994 is Wigan Bus Company Ikarus-bodied DAF SB220 (L533 EHD), which was only nine days old. (K. A. Jenkinson)

Looking smart and standing in Stockport bus station on 5 May 1994 is MTL Manchester's East Lancs-bodied Leyland Atlantean 1759 (MTJ 759S), which had started life with Merseyside PTE in September 1977. (K. A. Jenkinson)

Displaying a Baby Blue fleet name and seen here awaiting its passengers in Ashton-under-Lyne bus station in March 1994, is Pennine Blue Northern Counties-bodied Dodge S56 D974 TKC, which started life with Merseybus in March 1987. (B. Newsome)

Seen in Ashton-under-Lyne on 5 May 1994 is Northern Counties-bodied Iveco 49.10 F361 FNB, which was bought new by Mossley independent Tandy Bus in August 1988. Seen passing in the opposite direction and just peeping into the picture is two month-old Pennine Baby Blue Optare MetroRider 702 (L323 NRF). (K. A. Jenkinson)

Independent Tame Valley's ex-Merseyside PTE Leyland National SKF 26T rests between duties in Stockport bus station on 5 May 1994. (K. A. Jenkinson)

Seen in 1994 freshly painted in PMT's Pennine livery is ECW-bodied Bristol VRT DVL685 (YBF 685S), which was new to its parent in May 1978. (K. S. E. Till)

Leaving Oldham bus station at the start of its journey to Manchester in November 1995 is Alexander-bodied Volvo B6 310 (N750 PRS), which was new to Stagecoach Busways in October 1994 and was then loaned to Greater Manchester South shortly before its takeover by Stagecoach in February 1996. (B. Newsome)

Smartly painted in GM Buses North express livery, coach-bodied Northern Counties-bodied MCW Metrobus 5319 (D319 LNB) creeps out of Oldham Street into Market Street, Manchester, on 6 December 1995. (K. A. Jenkinson)

Heading along Chapel Street, Manchester, on 4 December 1995 is GM Buses North Northern Counties-bodied Leyland Atlantean 4486 (SND 486X), which began life with Greater Manchester PTE in January 1982. (K. A. Jenkinson)

Adorned with Superbus low floor branding, with added road dirt on its side panels, GM Buses North Wright-bodied Volvo B10B 505 (M505 PNA), which was new in January 1995, is seen in Chapel Street, Manchester, in December of that year. (K. A. Jenkinson)

New to Yorkshire Rider in March 1988, MCW Metrorider 1696 (E247 UWR) is seen here after being acquired by GM Buses North. (B. Newsome)

Loaned by West Midlands to Bee Line from 1992 to 1996 and repainted into its livery, MCW Metrobus 782 (BOK 52V), which was new in February 1980, is seen here in Piccadilly bus station, Manchester, on 4 December 1995. (K. A. Jenkinson)

Seen in Piccadilly, Manchester, on 4 December 1995 after being sold by Stagecoach to Finglands together with route 192 for which it carries branding, Alexander PS-bodied Volvo B10M 1419 (M419 RRN) was new to Ribble in October 1994 but was operated in Manchester from new. (K. A. Jenkinson)

Resting in Piccadilly bus station, Manchester, on 6 December 1995 is GM Buses South Express-liveried Northern Counties-bodied Leyland Olympian 3213 (C213 CBU). (K. A. Jenkinson)

Another ex-Greater Manchester PTE bus to remain in its home city after its sale, Northern Counties-bodied Daimler Fleetline 955 WAL, originally registered KBU 906P, is seen entering Piccadilly bus station on 4 December 1995 in service with local independent Walls of Fallowfield. (K. A. Jenkinson)

New in December 1988 to Walsh, Alkrington, who later rebranded itself JP Travel, Northern Counties-bodied Renault S46 F639 HVU is seen here in Ashton-under-Lyne bus station wearing City Nippy and Hail and Ride branding. (K. A. Jenkinson)

Also on loan from West Midlands to Bee Line from October 1994 to August 1996 and repainted into its later style livery is MCW Metrobus 797 (LOA 332X), seen here in Piccadilly bus station, Manchester, on 4 December 1995. (K. A. Jenkinson)

New to Merseyside PTE in August 1981, and seen here in Piccadilly bus station, Manchester, on 6 December 1995 operating for independent South Manchester, is somewhat battered Willowbrook-bodied Leyland Atlantean AFY 180X. (K. A. Jenkinson)

Having just deposited its passengers in Piccadilly bus station, Manchester, on 6 December 1995, Bullock of Cheadle's four-week-old Wright-bodied Scania L113CRL (N631 XBU) displays its easy access low-floor branding on its side and front panels. (K. A. Jenkinson)

GM Buses South Northern Counties-bodied Leyland Atlantean 4506 (SND 506X), seen here in Piccadilly bus station, Manchester, on 6 December 1995 displays a GMS logo in its front nearside upper-deck bulkhead window. (K. A. Jenkinson)

Another bus purchased new by Wigan Bus Company, Alexander (Belfast)-bodied Mercedes Benz 709D M385 KVR, which entered service in April 1994, is seen here in Wigan bus station on 23 March 1996. (B. Newsome)

Seen displaying Wigan Buses branding in March 1996 is GM Buses North one-year-old Northern Counties-bodied Dennis Dart 1103 (M103 RRJ). (B. Newsome)

New to Crosville in April 1983 and seen here in Wigan bus station on 23 March 1996 displaying a North Western Wigan Bus fleet name is Leyland National 2 282 (NTU 12Y). (B. Newsome)

Wearing PMT livery and Red Rider fleet names, ECW-bodied Leyland Olympian DOG799 (A170 VFM), which was new to Crosville in May 1984, leaves Stockport bus station on the 374 service to Hazel Grove station. (K. A. Jenkinson)

Standing in Bolton bus station in October 1996 is Timeline's Alexander (Belfast)-bodied Volvo B10L 303 (N303 WNF), which was new in November 1995. (K. A. Jenkinson)

Stagecoach's standard single-decker in the 1990s was the Alexander PS-bodied Volvo B10M, which was added to its fleets across the UK. Here, looking immaculate as it stands in its home city's Piccadilly bus station in September 1996, is Stagecoach Manchester's new 806 (N806 DNE). (K. A. Jenkinson)

Collecting its Macclesfield passengers in Piccadilly bus station, Manchester, on 17 September 1996, Stevenson's Alexander-bodied Leyland Olympian 1996 (F96 PRE) had been purchased new in December 1988. (K. S. E. Till)

Fronting a line of Stagecoach Manchester buses in Stockport bus station on September 1996 is Alexander-bodied Mercedes Benz 811D 413 (N413 WVR), which was new in November 1995. (K. A. Jenkinson)

Starting life with South Yorkshire PTE in August 1985, Optare-bodied Dennis Domino C41 HDT is seen here in Rochdale bus station on 12 October 1996 operated by local independent Pioneer. (K. S. E. Till)

Purchased new by Dennis's, Dukinfield, in February 1993, Dormobile-bodied Mercedes Benz 709D K287 ESF is seen here in Manchester city centre on 17 September 1996 awaiting its departure to Ashton-under-Lyne. (K. S. E. Till)

Only a few days old when photographed in Bolton bus station in December 1996 painted in First Greater Manchester livery with Superbus branding is Plaxton-bodied Dennis Dart SLF 6007 (P307 LND). (S. R. Procter)

With a body built/converted by its original operator PMT in September 1985, Mercedes Benz L608D MMM120 (C120 VBF) is seen here at Ashton-under-Lyne bus station wearing Red Rider fleet names. (B. Newsome)

Passing Bolton bus station on 7 March 1997, still wearing Greater Manchester PTE livery albeit with First Greater Manchester fleet names, is Northern Counties-bodied Leyland Fleetline 4108 (HDB 108V), which was new in December 1979. (K. A. Jenkinson)

With 'I'm a Little Gem' branding on its front roof dome and First Greater Manchester fleet name on its side panels, November 1986 vintage Northern Counties-bodied Dodge S56 1845 (D845 LND) prepares to enter Bolton bus station on 7 March 1997. (K. A. Jenkinson)

Passing Bolton bus station on its way to Manchester on the 25 service on 7 March 1997 despite carrying branding for the M10 service, is Stagecoach Ribble Alexander PS-bodied Volvo B10M 454 (M454 VCW). (K. A. Jenkinson)

Collecting its passengers in Bolton bus station on 7 March 1997 is independent Atherton Bus Company ECW-bodied Leyland Leopard CNH 171X, which had begun life with United Counties in March 1982. (K. A. Jenkinson)

Less than a month old, First Greater Manchester North Wright-bodied Volvo B10BLE 571 (R571 YNC) gathers up its passengers in Wigan bus station on 30 August 1997. (K. S. E. Till)

Resting at the Eccles terminus of the 15 service to Manchester in December 1987 is London Transport AEC Routemaster RM572 (WLT 572), which was on loan for two months to local independent Blue Bus for evaluation. (K. A. Jenkinson)

Branded for the Nottingham to Manchester Trans Peak service, Trent Alexander (Belfast)-bodied Volvo B10M 53 (M53 PRA), which was new in November 1994, collects its passengers in Stockport bus station in October 1998. (K. A. Jenkinson)

New to West Yorkshire PTE in October 1984 and seen here on the north side of Piccadilly in November 1998 after its transfer to First Manchester, MCW Metrobus 5562 (B562 RWY) has been repainted into 'tomato soup' livery. (K. A. Jenkinson)

Seen in Stockport bus station on the National Express 540 service from London to Rochdale in October 1998 is Van Hool-bodied Volvo B10M LSK 870, which was new to Park, Hamilton. (K. A. Jenkinson)

New to Bullock, Cheadle, in March 1998, Optare Spectra-bodied DAF DB250 (R291 CVM), which was the first low-floor double-deck bus in Manchester, is seen here parked outside Stockport bus station in November of that same year. (K. A. Jenkinson)

Having just arrived at Stockport bus station on the 199 service from Buxton on 20 March 1998 is Trent Optare-bodied MAN 11.190 809 (M809 PRA), which was purchased new in November 1994. In June 2005 it was donated to the Asia Bus Response and exported to Indonesia following the disastrous tsunami. (K. A. Jenkinson)

Awaiting departure from Stockport bus station on the 401 express service to Bolton in November 1998 is First Manchester North's 'tomato soup' liveried Wright-bodied Volvo B10B 512 (M512 PNA), which was new in February 1995. (K. A. Jenkinson)

Displaying a Pennine fleet name, First PMT Plaxton-bodied Mercedes Benz 709D MMM410 (N410 HVT), which was new in June 1996, stands between duties in Stockport bus station in November 1998. (K. A. Jenkinson)

Starting life with Stagecoach Sussex Coastline in February 1994, and seen here in Stockport bus station on the X1 service to Derby in November 1998 after its transfer to Stagecoach Manchester South, is Plaxton Paramount-bodied Dennis Javelin 1107 (L107 SDY). (K. A. Jenkinson)

Seen in Altrincham Interchange in November 1998 while working a 16A duty to Manchester and displaying 'Arriva serving the North West' lettering is ECW-bodied Leyland Olympian 2162 (B962 WRN), which began life with Ribble in February 1985. (M. H. A. Flynn)

Carrying Warrington Gold Line fleet names, North Western Plaxton-bodied Dennis Dart 1212 (M212 YKD) is seen here at Altrincham Interchange in November 1998 preparing for a return journey to its home town. (K. A. Jenkinson)

Still wearing the livery of its former owner, Timeline, but displaying Arriva fleet names, Alexander (Belfast)-bodied Mercedes Benz 709D 163 (P183 FNF) is seen here entering Altrincham Interchange in November 1998. (K. A. Jenkinson)

Seen here in Piccadilly bus station, Manchester, on the 263 service to Altrincham in November 1998, is immaculately presented North Western Bee Line East Lancs-bodied Dennis Falcon H 383 (G383 EKA), which was new in May 1990. (K. A. Jenkinson)

Heading along Portland Street, Manchester, on its way to Rochdale, and displaying Easyride fleet names, is Rossendale Transport Plaxton-bodied Dennis Dart SPD 119 (S119 KRN). (M. H. A. Flynn)

Still painted in Greater Manchester Buses livery but having received First Manchester logos, standing in Piccadilly bus station in November 1998 is Northern Counties-bodied Leyland Fleetline 4988 (DWH 704W), which began life with PTE subsidiary Lancashire United in December 1980. (K. A. Jenkinson)

Seen in Piccadilly bus station, Manchester, awaiting its departure to Macclesfield in November 1998, is Stevenson's Wright-bodied Leyland Swift 1131 (J31 SFA), which had been purchased new in December 1991. (K. A. Jenkinson)

Picking its Buxton-bound passengers up in Stockport bus station en route from Manchester Airport in November 1998 and wearing Skyline branding, Trent's Optare-bodied MAN 11.190 812 (M812 PRA), like its sister seen earlier, was exported to Indonesia as part of the Asia Bus Response in June 2005. (K. A. Jenkinson)

Collecting a healthy load of passengers in Piccadilly bus station, Manchester, in November 1998, is Stagecoach Manchester South long wheelbase Alexander-bodied Volvo Olympian 718 (P718 GND), which was new to the company in October 1996. (K. A. Jenkinson)

Entering Altrincham Interchange in November 1998 is Arriva North West Alexander (Belfast)-bodied Mercedes Benz 709D (M363 KVR), which was new to Arrowline (Star Line), Knutsford, in April 1995. (K. A. Jenkinson)

Sporting 'Arriva serving the north Midlands' fleet name, Wadham Stringer-bodied Leyland Swift 1148 (E993 NMK), which was new to Armchair, Brentford, in April 1988, is seen in Piccadilly bus station, Manchester, in October 1998, awaiting its Macclesfield-bound passengers. (K. A. Jenkinson)

Pictured at Altrincham Interchange in November 1998 when only a few months old is Arriva's Alexander-bodied Dennis Dart SOF 1303 (R303 CVU), which carries route branding for the Skyline service to Manchester Airport. (M. H. A. Flynn)

Resting at Altrincham Interchange in November 1998 are Arriva Manchester Alexander-bodied Dennis Dart SLF 1310 (R310 CVU) and ex-Timeline Alexander (Belfast)-bodied Mercedes Benz 709D 161 (M166 LNC), while leaving for the airport is First Manchester North Plaxton-bodied Dennis Dart SLF 6011 (P311 LND). (K. A. Jenkinson)

With a sign inside the bottom of its windscreen stating 'this is a no smoking bus' – obviously relating to passengers rather than its exhaust – North Western Bee Line East Lancs-bodied Dennis Falcon H 390 (B51 XFV), seen here at Altrincham Interchange in November 1998, had started life with municipality-owned Hyndburn in February 1985. (K. A. Jenkinson)

Departing Altrincham Interchange on the 263 service to Manchester Piccadilly in November 1998 is North Western Bee Line Leyland National 2 271 (VBG 89V), which had been new to Merseyside PTE in June 1980. (K. A. Jenkinson)

Sporting a Firstbus logo, Pennine fleet name, and Localine branding, Northern Counties-bodied Renault S75 MRP533 (H722 CNC), which was new to Greater Manchester PTE in September 1990, is seen here in Stockport bus station in December 1998. (K. A. Jenkinson)

Passing through Stockport bus station in December 1998 is First Potteries PMT Knype-bodied Leyland Swift E342 NFA, which started life as a demonstrator in April 1998. (K. A. Jenkinson)

Bullock of Cheadle's Leyland National 2 JIL 8216, seen here at Altrincham Interchange in December 1998, started life with PMT in February 1984 registered A301 JFA. (K. A. Jenkinson)

Stagecoach Manchester South's low-cost Magic Bus Northern Counties-bodied Leyland Olympian 3002 (ANA 2Y), adorned with branding for route 192, is seen here in Piccadilly, Manchester, in December 1998. (K. A. Jenkinson)

Travelling along Market Street, Manchester, in December 1998, Bluebird of Middleton's East Lancs-bodied Dennis Dart SLF S551 BNV, which was purchased new in August 1998, still wears its dealer stock white livery. (K. A. Jenkinson)

Preparing to leave Stockport bus station in December 1998 on the X67 service to Chesterfield for which it is branded, is Staveley-based independent Ringwood Luxury Coaches two-month-old Mellor-bodied Mercedes Benz 0814D S276 LGA. (K. A. Jenkinson)

Seen in Manchester on 10 June 1999 on the 135 service for which it carries branding, First Manchester's Wright-bodied Volvo B10LA bendibus 2004 (S994 UJA) was new in March of that year. (A. Blagburn)

Resting in the yard of its owner, Coachmasters of Rochdale, on 22 September 1999, is immaculately presented Plaxton Paramount 3500-bodied Volvo B10M WLT 697, which began life with Western Scottish in May 1985 registered B197 CGA. (K. A. Jenkinson)

Carrying route branding for the 313 service above its side windows, Stagecoach Manchester Alexander-bodied MAN 18.220 101 (S101 TRJ), which was new in November 1998, is pictured here in Stockport bus station on 22 May 2000. (K. A. Jenkinson)

Seen in Stockport on the X1 service to Derby on 22 May 2000 is First PMT Leyland Lynx 852 (H852 GRE), which was new to the company in August 1990. (K. A. Jenkinson)

Another bus adorned with Skyline branding, Stagecoach Manchester South Alexander-bodied MAN 18.220 152 (S152 TRJ) stands in Stockport bus station on 22 May 2000 awaiting its departure to Manchester Airport. (K. A. Jenkinson)

Built in May 1992 as a demonstrator for its manufacturer, unique Alexander-bodied Iveco 480-12-21 Turbocity J227 OKX is seen here at Bluebird's Middleton depot on 10 September 2000 alongside V4 BLU, an East Lancs-bodied Scania N113DRB, which had also started life as a demonstrator. (K. A. Jenkinson)

Resting at its Middleton depot on Sunday 10 September 2000 are Bluebird Marshall-bodied Iveco 40.19 R15 BLU and UVG-bodied Mercedes Benz 0814 R18 BLU. (K. A. Jenkinson)

Purchased new by Bluebird, Middleton, in June 1997, Wright-bodied Dennis Dart SLF 50 (P50 BLU) is seen here at its owner's depot on 10 September 2000. (K. A. Jenkinson)

Seen at Middleton depot on 10 September 2000 while on hire to Bluebird from Nottingham City Transport is East Lancs-bodied Scania L113CRL 640 (P640 ENN), which was new in November 1996. (K. A. Jenkinson)

Purchased for spares by Bluebird, Middleton, and seen here at its Middleton depot on 10 September 2000 is former London United MCW Metrobus M138 (BYX 138V), while alongside it is Alexander-bodied Leyland Leopard driver trainer OSJ 610R, which started life with Western SMT in December 1976, and former Kelvin Scottish Alexander-bodied MCW Metrobus D682 MHS. (K. A. Jenkinson)

Standing outside its owner's Princess Road depot on 10 September 2000 is Stagecoach Manchester South's Magic Bus-liveried Duple Metsec-bodied tri-axle Dennis Dragon 695 (M695 MDB), which had been imported from Stagecoach Kenya to whom it had been supplied new in 1996. (K. A. Jenkinson)

Seen at its depot on 10 September 2000 when only a few days old is Finglands Plaxton-bodied Volvo B7TL 1762 (X762 ABU) adorned with low floor lettering. (K. A. Jenkinson)

Also seen at Finglands' Fallowfield depot on 10 September 2000, is Alexander-bodied Volvo Olympian 1740 (N740 VBA), which had been purchased new in August 1995. (K. A. Jenkinson)

Another of Finglands' buses seen at its Fallowfield depot on 10 September 2000 is former Stagecoach Ribble (Manchester) Alexander PS-bodied Volvo B10M-55 M422 RRN, freshly repainted from Stagecoach stripes into its new owner's livery with new fleet number 1422. (K. A. Jenkinson)

Still wearing the livery of its previous owner, independent Rochdale-based Coachmasters, but with First Manchester Schools logos, East Lancs-bodied Scania N113DRB 4806 (H812 WKH), seen here near Rochdale on 31 January 2001, started life with Kingston upon Hull City Transport in September 1990. (K. A. Jenkinson)

Resting in Stockport bus station on 15 May 2002 are First Manchester Alexander-bodied Volvo B0M-50 7047 (G690 PNS), which began life with Strathclyde Buses in November 1989 and is seen here in First's step-entrance livery, and Wright-bodied Volvo B10B 554 (N554 WVR), which was new to GM Buses North in February 1996. (K. A. Jenkinson)

Decorated with branding for Manchester's free city centre bus services, and seen here at Piccadilly railway station in the late summer of 2002, is First Manchester Optare M850 Solo 40335 (ML02 OGE), which was new in July of that year. (M. H. A. Flynn)

Purchased new by Finglands, Fallowfield, in September 1999, Mercedes Benz 0405N 1428 (V428 DNB) proudly displays its low floor credentials as it stands in Piccadilly bus station, Manchester, on 15 May 2002. (K. A. Jenkinson)

New to independent Dennis's in November 1997, and branded for the route connecting Manchester city centre with the Sportcity Stadium, Plaxton-bodied Dennis Dart SLF R575 ABA is seen here en route to Ashton-under-Lyne on 15 May 2002. (K. A. Jenkinson)

Heading to Manchester's Arndale Centre on 15 May 2002 is JP Travel's Plaxton-bodied Dennis Dart SLF P876 PWW, which was new to Manchester Airport in March 1997. Behind it is UK North Alexander-bodied DAF DB250 V654 LWT, which had been purchased new in September 1999. (K. A. Jenkinson)

Carrying branding for the XVII Commonweath Games and lettered 'Team Bus', new First Leicester Wright-bodied Volvo B7L 315 (KV02 VVX) is seen here approaching Manchester Piccadilly railway station on 15 May 2002 while on loan to First Manchester for the aforementioned event. (K. A. Jenkinson)

Standing in Piccadilly bus station, Manchester, on 15 May 2002 is Stagecoach Manchester South Alexander-bodied long wheelbase Volvo Olympian 781 (S781 RVU), which was new in August 1998 and is seen repainted into its owner's new beach ball livery. (K. A. Jenkinson)

Illustrating Stagecoach's old and new liveries, Stagecoach Manchester Alexander-bodied MAN 18.220s 233 (X233 BNE) and 132 (S132 TRJ) are both seen here operating the 192 service to Stockport on 15 May 2002. (K. A. Jenkinson)

Starting life with London Buses in July 1980, MCW Metrobus BYX 302V was, in November 2000, sold to Ensign, Purfleet, who two years later converted it to open top for use on its new City Sightseeing operation in Manchester where it is seen here on 15 May 2002. (K. A. Jenkinson)

Withdrawn in the yard of Stagecoach Manchester's Stockport depot on 15 May 2002 are ECW-bodied Bristol LH6L former driver trainers TV09 (VDV 105S) and TV11 (YAE 516V), which began life with Western National and Bristol Omnibus Co. respectively. (K. A. Jenkinson)

Leaving Stockport bus station on the circular route 380 on 15 May 2002 is independent Ashall's Plaxton-bodied Dennis Dart SLF V390 HGG, which was purchased new by its owner in January 2000. (K. A. Jenkinson)

Leaving Stockport bus station on a short journey to its nearby depot on 15 May 2002 is Stagecoach Manchester Alexander PS-bodied Volvo B10M 855 (P855 GND), which was new to the company in October 1996. (K. A. Jenkinson)

Travelling along Wilmslow Road, Manchester, on 15 May 2002 is UK North's ex-London Selkent/Stagecoach Leyland Titan T823 (A823 SUL), which was new in August 1983, acquired by UK North in February 2001, and sold in June 2002. (K. A. Jenkinson)

New to China Motor Bus, Hong Kong, in December 1993, and reimported by First PMT in 2000, Alexander-bodied tri-axle Leyland Olympian 3010 (K480 EUX) is seen here in its new home city on 15 May 2002 after being transferred to First Manchester. (K. A. Jenkinson)

Painted in the Queen's Golden Jubilee livery, Stagecoach Manchester South Alexander-bodied Dennis Trident 1627 (MK02 EGV), which was new in April 2002, is seen here leaving East Didsbury terminus on its return journey to Manchester on 15 May 2002. (K. A. Jenkinson)

Collecting its passengers on the XV11 Commonwealth Games stadium shuttle service on 15 May 2002 when only a few weeks old is Stagecoach Manchester Alexander-bodied Dennis Trident 1629 (MK02 EGY), which carries front and side branding for the operation. (K. A. Jenkinson)

Starting life fitted with a Duple Dominant bus body with West Yorkshire PTE in June 1983 registered EWR 657Y, Blue Bus Leyland Tiger 74 (WJI 9074) was given its new East Lancs body in January 1999, and is seen here in Bolton on 2 August 2002. (K. A. Jenkinson)

Despite carrying branding above its side windows for route 534, Blue Bus Alexander-bodied Dennis Dart SLF 15 (MF51 TVV), which had been purchased new in January 2002 and displays a Blue Buggy Bus name on its front panel, is seen here eight months later leaving Bolton bus station on the 528 service to Belmont. (K. A. Jenkinson)

Seen here in Bolton bus station on 2 August 2002 carrying branding for the 225 service to Clitheroe is Lancashire United Wright-bodied Volvo B10BLE 1076 (Y176 HRN), which was new to the company in August 2001. (K. A. Jenkinson)

Having been sold to Lancashire United but seen here in Bolton bus station on 2 August 2002 still sporting Stagecoach livery, albeit with its new owner's fleet names, is Alexander-bodied Dennis Lance J116 WSC, which was new to London Buses in dual-door format in June 1992, and passed to Blue Bus, Bolton, in 2003. (K. A. Jenkinson)

Looking immaculate as it stands at its owner's Atherton depot on 5 April 2003 is South Lancs Travel's Alexander (Belfast)-bodied Leyland Tiger G59 RND, which had started life with Shearings in October 1989. (K. A. Jenkinson)

New to Bristol Omnibus Co. in April 1980 and later operating for Badgerline, ECW-bodied Bristol LH6L AFB 597V was acquired by South Lancs Travel in February 1991. Later, in 1998 it was loaned to MK Metro, Milton Keynes, and repainted into its livery before returning to South Lancs in 2002. Seen here at its rightful owner's Atherton depot on 5 April 2003, it was ultimately sold for preservation in 2012. (K. A. Jenkinson)

Standing in the bus wash at its owner's depot on 5 April 2003 is South Lancs Travel East Lancs-bodied Volvo B10M-50 H678 GPF, which was new to London Country South West in December 1990. (K. A. Jenkinson)

Passing through Bolton on 5 April 2003 is Blue Bus all-Leyland Olympian 119 (H549 GKX), which began life in London in January 1991 with Armchair, Brentford, before reaching its new northern home in August 2002. (K. A. Jenkinson)

New to Blackburn Corporation in October 1982, Middleton-based independent M. R. Travel's well-presented East Lancs-bodied Leyland Atlantean VBV 22Y was twenty-one years old when seen here in Rochdale bus station on 3 June 2003. (K. A. Jenkinson)

M. R. Travel's much travelled Plaxton-bodied Dennis Dart SLF V946 DNB, which began life with Trent in February 2000, prepares to leave Rochdale bus station on local service 448 to Wardle on 3 June 2003 displaying 'Your local service for Rochdale' on its foremost side panel. (K. A. Jenkinson)

Local independent Bu-Val Buses Mellor-bodied Iveco 59.12 805 (R805 WJA), which had been purchased new in December 1997, is seen here resting between duties in Rochdale bus station on 3 June 2003. (K. A. Jenkinson)

Starting life with Grampian Regional Transport, Mercedes Benz 0405 60430 (M524 RSS) is seen here in Rochdale bus station on 3 June 2003 after its transfer to First Manchester. (K. A. Jenkinson)

New to Stagecoach, Kenya, in 1996, and reimported to the UK in 1998, despite wearing Megabus branding following its withdrawal from these long-distance duties, Stagecoach Manchester's Duple Met Sec-bodied tri-axle Dennis Dragon M680 TDB was used on local bus services as seen here in Piccadilly bus station, Manchester, on 19 November 2004. (K. A. Jenkinson)

Purchased new by Dennis's, Dukinfield, in October 2000, East Lancs-bodied Dennis Trident X792 JHG, seen here at Piccadilly, Manchester, on 19 November 2004, passed to Stagecoach Manchester upon its acquisition of the independent operator in 2005. (K. A. Jenkinson)

Passing through Manchester on a Megabus service to London on 19 November 2004 is Jonckheere Monaco-bodied MAN 24.359 50048 (T48 BBW), which began life with Thames Transit in July 1999 operating the London Tube service from Oxford. (K. A. Jenkinson)

Representing First Manchester's second generation bendibuses for operation on the 135 service, for which it is branded, is Scania N94UA 12009 (YN05 GYG), which is seen here in May 2005 when only a month old. (M. H. A. Flynn)

Reimported to the UK by Stagecoach from Kowloon Motor Bus, Hong Kong, in 2004, Stagecoach Manchester Magic Bus-liveried Alexander-bodied tri-axle Leyland Olympian 13513 (C38 HNF), seen here on 5 April 2005, was new in February 1986. (M. H. A. Flynn)

Passing Altrincham Interchange on 20 May 2005 is Eccles-based Go Goodwins Optare Excel WSV 553, which was new to British Telecom, Goonhilly, in April 1997 registered P915SUM. (M. H. A. Fynn)

Painted in Stagecoach Manchester's driver training livery is Northern Counties-bodied Leyland Olympian 13272 (D272 JVR), which was new in December 1986 to Greater Manchester Buses. (M. H. A. Flynn)

Arriving at Altrincham Interchange displaying a MidiLines name on its front panel is Warrington Borough Transport Marshall-bodied Dennis Dart 248 (M248 YWM), which was new to the undertaking in June 1995. (M. H. A. Flynn)

Sale independent LA Coaches Optare M850 Solo MX06 ABZ, which was bought new in April 2006, is seen here heading to Wythenshawe Hospital on route 178. (M. H. A. Flynn)

Seen here in Altrincham on the 37 service to its home town, Warrington, on 29 June 2006, is independent Bennetts Duple-bodied Dennis Dart H101 VFV, which began life with Rossendale Transport in August 1990. (M. H. A. Flynn)

New in March 2005 and seen here carrying Oxford Road Link branding is Bullock of Cheadle's Scania N94UB YN05 GZZ, behind which is Stagecoach Manchester's Magic Bus-liveried Alexander-bodied Leyland Olympian 16759 (D759 DRJ), which began life with Greater Manchester South in June 1998. (M. H. A. Flynn)

Arriving in Manchester on 16 September 2006 on the non-stop service from Liverpool, for which it is branded, is Stansted-based Terravison's Irizar-bodied Scania K114IB4 (YN04 YJK), which was new in June 2004. (M. H. A. Flynn)

Seen in Manchester Piccadilly on the 44 service to Gatley on 16 June 2008, Hayton's four-week-old Plaxton-bodied Enterprise KX08OLC stands in front of Bullock's East Lancs-bodied Dennis Trident W672PTD. (M. H. A. Flynn)